THERE IS ANOTHER POEM,

IN WHICH THE NEWS

IS ERASED AND REWRITTEN

🌿

ZACHARY HARRIS

THERE IS ANOTHER POEM,

IN WHICH THE NEWS

IS ERASED AND REWRITTEN

☙

ZACHARY HARRIS

NEW MICHIGAN PRESS
TUCSON, ARIZONA

NEW MICHIGAN PRESS
DEPT OF ENGLISH, P. O. BOX 210067
UNIVERSITY OF ARIZONA
TUCSON, AZ 85721-0067

<http://newmichiganpress.com/nmp>

Orders and queries to nmp@thediagram.com.

Copyright © 2010 by Zachary Harris.
All rights reserved.

ISBN 978-1-934832-28-8. FIRST PRINTING.

Printed in the United States of America.

Design by Ander Monson.

Cover image: "Night Sky, Vermont", photo by Lillian-Yvonne Bertram.

CONTENTS

Palinode   1

De proprietatibus rerum   3
    Musical Theatre   5
    Ekberg, Anita   6
    Cervus   8
    Cameron, Julia Margaret   9
    Defeat   10
    Him   11
    The Adriatic Sea   12
    Levis, Larry   13
    Panic   14
    Hibernation   15
    Samson   17
    One   18
    Vesper   19

Piss Clams: An Unnatural History   21

Gospels   34

Notes   39
Acknowledgments   41

PALINODE

In the age of malformed tools
I was mistaken to think I was a man.
Would a man lope beside the loping river.
Would a man shatter the neck of a chicken just to see
If he could perceive the honesty of its death. Would a man know
How dearly torches look like eyes as they float above the river.
Would a man become hollow with wishes. Would a man lie in pieces
In the garret of a dead building. Would a man leave hands of clay on
Everything he loves. Would a man bear terror like a fine coat.
Would a man never have had anything to bruise. Would a man be
Without anything between his legs. Would a man try
To fill that absence by sinking into his earth
A cherry switch, unlit candle,
A crescent of dead bees.

De proprietatibus rerum,
or On the Properties of Things

MUSICAL THEATRE

A play with music. When one is watching a piece of musical theatre, one is watching a shattering approximation of reality. Musicals may be sung-through or they may be composed of songs with interstitial speaking. Speaking, as such, is dead. Many musicals are about love. An equal number are about death. What few are then left belong to animals, or forgetting. Musical theatre is interior. It is, as such, concerned with blood and transportation. Often it will seem as though someone is singing for no reason. This is rarely the case. What recourse does a woman in love with a horse, or a man in love with a man, or a ghost in love with a child have besides singing. The horse has a lovely baritone the color of molasses. The child does not. Musical theatre is considered by many to be a liminal art, and is therefore very dear to homosexuals. Perhaps it is the sequins or the proximity to women with strong eyebrows.

_____, widely considered to be the first "modern" musical, begins with an all-girl chorus line and ends with the horse underneath a ghost light. Only its most distinct features are visible. The light covers its head like a fine powder. It is singing lowly, sweetly, from far within its bellows. There is another voice, unidentified.

EKBERG, ANITA

"I had a dream where I was a mountaineer. After tying the most elaborate

Knots, I set out. I thought that maybe it was a volcano, but when I got to the

Top, I realized I had been scaling my own breasts. That was when I woke up.

I thought, for just a moment, that I was still in Sweden, still in those mouth-

Like and barren fjords. Always those dead frogs with their strange smiles. But

I could see from the awful bed that I was in Roma—dear Roma. I felt like a

Coin with its glamour rubbed away. Like the first time a horse threw me, back

In the Canyon. How lovely & red those hills. How nothing like Sweden. I really

Knew how to waste time then: On horses. I dream about them all the time.

Sometimes they have the heads of handsome men, and I
   ride them up a hill

That we discover is, again & again, Sweden. But I have
   always been

Disappointed. I was like this as a baby. Mother always
   said I was

Inconsolable when the garden, done for the season,
   died."

CERVUS

Those Iranian pastoralists, the Scythians (see: *Departed Civilizations*), welcomed deer as mystical protectors of the dead. They darted between this world and the next, or other, as easily as crossing a country road. This is not all that easy. They are often found dead, so they are suggestive of a condition. Whether this condition is a palimpsest of the human condition (or vice versa) or not is currently unknown. What is known: One came near enough to touch. It strayed out from the tree-line, slowly, as though through dark water. It was elegant in a hopeless way, carrying the shock of the moon on its gut. The doe—that's what it was, a doe, not a germ of antler on her skull—stepped nimbly into the road. Whatever she was, she was only one hundred pounds of it when the car, coming fast, split her like an envelope. This is not inauspicious; her coiled madnesses are meant to be read. But by whom. By what light.

CAMERON, JULIA MARGARET

A Victorian photographer famous for her portraits. She interred herself in the heart of the forest. She hounded the beauty that she herself was denied. She had many sisters. Each of them had a nickname such as Beauty. Julia's nickname was Talent. The photographic technique of which she was fondest resulted in a soft focus and scratches through which light falls as though the image itself were obscuring some thing of light. Her portraits were of friends, many of whom were notables of the day, or else tableaux reproducing famous allegorical paintings. This is the angel in the water. This is the child bride holding the fat bird of morning. Various female relations sat for her. Because Julia wanted to capture them at their most natural, she encouraged them to let their hair down. This had the effect of making them look like women. In the heart of the forest, she worked in a small studio. Her hands all day in trays of silver, always. The hounds of beauty at her feet.

DEFEAT

> *Our efforts are those of men prone to disaster;*
> *our efforts are like those of the Trojans.*

It is easy to visit defeat upon me; I am vain, and shallow. Mostly I am weak the waterlogged piece. You were a snake and I was skinless and swam into your gullet. Our dreams hinged like a Venn diagram, and created that space of abject pity. What a day that was, to quote from The Talking Heads. Also apt would be ABBA, who sang of the tender saber of Waterloo, as in, there are small Waterloos sewn into the lining of my coat. They belch and climb like flies. I had nothing keeping me in. I was appalled by my own helplessness. But I am easily appalled. We were both of us smaller than ourselves. We bent the scorched grass but willingly. In the red car we went to state parks and found things. You killed an owl or we both did. Its paper skull sat on my sill for months after, for love. I threw it away; the snows of my exile swallowed the window.

HIM

The objective form of the third-person singular pronoun *he*. Have you seen him. Him and I were supposed to go on a picnic. I have accused him. I am accusing him. Him is not the subject. Him is not quite an object either. Him is alive, him has all of his parts, him is breathing. Him is very smart. Him makes fried chicken. Him is very particular. In this way, him may be an object. There is nothing objective about him. I have felt him. I am feeling him. Him reads many books, most of which are written in dead languages. Thus, each book is like a sepulcher for him to unseal. Him is not a dead language. Him is not a sepulcher. Him is very much alive. I have read him. I am reading him. Him has such stories to tell. Him is a wishing-well. Him produces such sensations. Thus, him is a subject of my body. Him is a goat astray. Him cut a hole. I cut a hole in him. Into these holes we mislaid our footing. I am asking him. I asked him to go. Him went.

THE ADRIATIC SEA

A bell-shrouded town; town around a steeple, strafed
   with doleful sunlight; a jellyfish

Looming at the tide; a string of widows climbing the
   hill; the hem of their weeds and the

Gold dust daubed there; the breast of each town;
   tessellating dusky roof town; the raucous

Game of the sea-birds; fall asleep town; gray light at
   dawn; son slipping into the church; a

Quarrel of boats limned with salt, their hulls touching
   and pulling apart; north wind and

South wind town; the alley becoming a window; bells
   go; a tower sparrow dives everywhere;

The cacti with not a needle; town-of-the-oldest-pines;
   bullet hole town; the flat rock for

Inscription from the sea; olives that fatten even in the
   winter; I looked into one and it gazed

Back like a dark window

LEVIS, LARRY

Larry Levis was a horse man. That is, above all other animals, he derived succor from the horse. There was one horse, in particular, a black horse that Larry did not comfort with a name. He rode this horse through a strange and ruined America. Here is Larry among the vineyard racks, naked and trembling for the winter. Here is Larry in a men's room. Here is Larry making love to a blue flame. Before his untimely death, Larry wrote a number of poems. Larry Levis died of a heart attack. That is, he became engorged with the wild significances of the banal. Larry read his life as most might read a newspaper. Larry Levis often thought of his hand as separate from his body and its processes. That is, his hand was so bound to his body and its processes that it seemed to move of its own accord. Despite his death, Larry still comes to the utterly alone. Say, off the road, there is a barn. This barn has an open door. Through the door is a man brushing, as though against a current, a black horse. The black horse looks nameless.

PANIC

Irrational thought is a currency in the age of fear. This was preceded by the age of geometrics, which was itself preceded by the age of malformed tools. Before that, records are largely oral. Panic is not reserved, as so much is, for man. A hard shine has been observed in packs of animals. This is panic. Trees have been known, in autumn, to cough once and die. This too is panic. One may sweat. One's breathing may become a labor. One may formulate contracts, none of which could possibly be fulfilled to the satisfaction of all parties. If a river, then we must not move against it. Especially insidious is the panic of blankness. Imagine a sheet of paper, and placing oneself on it. There is nothing, and it is perpetual. It is like the moon, or as after a deep snowfall. One could go this way: desperate for the borders of that country.

HIBERNATION

The most famous hibernators are Bears (see: *The Bear*).
Many will be familiar

With the sight of a bear wrestling with incredulity. This
bear is often accompanied

By smaller bears, just as a man is often accompanied by
smaller men who bear

His phobias to the public sphere. This sphere is bright
and vacant, and to escape it,

A man must gather up his emissaries and climb into a
winter maw. There, he can

And will cover himself with soft roots and leaves, and
sleep for a season. The season

That passes is one of degradation. There is no human
need to record it. The word

Hibernation could mean *winter-state*. But when
hibernating, sleep means very

Different things for a man and a bear. A bear actually
sleeps, and will not rouse itself

To eat or rid itself of waste. A man will sleep, but a man
   may also debase himself.

A bear will stop just through the gates of sleep. A man
   will not. A man

Will seek something deeper. A man will take
   hibernation as his

Crest. A man will wear this helmet into the ground.

SAMSON

"I took the lion. It was taken. I placed one hand on
his jaw and the other on his genitals and he split like a
soft fruit. His inside ferocious with light. I carried the
carcass on my back. My other back. We passed fields of
sentient hives, fondled by darkness. On the third day,
the carcass began to murmur. I set it down. I sat down
near the cleft. Separating the folds, I found a small
state of bees. They had forced the light into honey. The
impossibility failed to register with me, or the bees, or
the lion who had been set to an impossible sleep. The
honey was the thickest. I ate it by the handful. We all of
us came to a mess on the road. When D undoes her self,
that honey comes back to me."

ONE

A number, and the name of the glyph representing that number. This is strange, as one usually does not think of the quantity and the glyph as separate, as though one were the body and one were *the body*. In this way, it seems that one is two. But one is not two. Zero comes before one. Like zero, one is empty. Thus, it contains much. The glyph was first written, perpendicular to how we imagine it now, in India. There are many crocuses in India. It is debatable whether this had any effect on the glyph. The glyph became erect over time, and a chart of its development resembles the evolution of man. The quantity, on the other hand, has always been with us. One tree brings much needed perspective to the idea of the horizon. Humans only possess one of each organ, with the exception of the kidney, the lung, the gonad, and small common glands. The ideal of our time is to be by oneself. Imagine a plain, with a solitary man standing in the middle. There may be a scrub needle, or a hillock, or a man-made lake. But there is only one man. He knows about himself. He knows that he does not know himself. One bird, a wide dark thing, crosses overhead.

VESPER

James Wright the American Poet wrote extensively on
 the phenomenology of evening. It

makes fresh the body of each thing, inching down the
 street like a big car. Like influenza, it

kills the young or weak. However, this death is not to be
 of the body. In his journal entry of

April 7, 1973, 7:12 p.m., Wright wrote *the creek is
 mumbled with American ducks, they wear green*

*rings around their necks, their necks which are thin and
 breakable*. They would have been easy prey

for crows, which are themselves an imprecise metonymy
 for evening. Wright once stumbled

upon a crow that had been eaten by a big cat. Only its
 beak was left, and it told him all about

crow life, how small and murderous. Every one creature
 is deformed by fear. In his journal

entry of August 19, 1966, 7:35 p.m., Wright the Gentle
    Horse-Breaker wrote *I & the one I*

love can not recognize each other in the evening—

PISS CLAMS: AN UNNATURAL HISTORY

A soft-shell clam that is too large for its shell, and therefore must exhibit its siphon. They were collected on the North Shore of Long Island by Doris, my grandmother, and Flo, my great-aunt, during occasional visits to the area. They waited right at the waterline, in shackles of water.

PISS CLAMS & I

Nobody remembers. So the cabin, with its dark airs, squatted behind a sand dune, its hide studded with wild eyes of sea-rocket. Each bedroom had a window with a view of more sand. Sometimes they found palm-sized white crabs wrapped up in their blankets. Sometimes they heard the gulls vomiting all night.

PISS CLAMS: AN EROTICS

After she pulled the clam out like a sick tooth, Flo got pissed on. Doris laughed and laughed, and wanted to remember the arc of the clear liquor and the light behind and within the arc. They sat down on a flat rock, and Flo removed a tiny knife from her pocket. Placing it between her thumb and forefinger, she wrestled the tip into the clam's seam. Cracking open the shell, she turned it to Doris, who regarded the meat—alien, dun-colored— before placing it, whole, in her mouth.

PISS CLAMS & I

Jerry and Sam, the girls' husbands, had both been in the war. Jerry had been in the European Theatre, Sam, the Pacific. They still talked about it, as they turned cards over late into the night. Their responsibility with regard to the clams was to melt the salt pork into silk. Once that was done, they listened to the tin roof twisting in the sea air, which reminded them of the settling of metal that is the lullaby of warlife. They loved their wives, deeply.

PISS CLAMS: THE B-MOVIE

In the middle of the night, they lifted themselves out of the sand with their thick feet. The moonlight was clear-minded. They pulled themselves toward the sand dunes as if they were one giant mind. Their slightly parted shells shone with a menacing red glow. Doris watched as they crested the dune and tumbled toward the porch. She narrowed her eyes, muttered something to herself, and cocked the shotgun.

PISS CLAMS & I

Flo and Doris tied their hair up in scarves, and gingerly stepped onto the beach. Everything around them was silvered. Doris carried a bucket of hammered tin, sky-blue, and Flo carried the matching shovel. Flo was the Digger, the steady-hands. Doris couldn't stomach the action.

PISS CLAMS: LOVE LASTS FOREVER

Jerry's hair was never longer than at the shore. It just grew and grew, sometimes right around Doris's finger. He said it was the sea air, all those vitamins. She suggested that maybe it was the clams—how much courage they must have had to live in their own tombs. They were standing right at the waterline as the sun's acetylene slicked across the water toward them. A few feet away, a crab lay on its back, its soft stomach a comfort for the gulls. Doris felt a watery happiness. Jerry kissed her just as the light on the beach went out.

PISS CLAMS & I

Jerry and Sam rarely spoke, though they usually sat together at the lame card table by the stove. They had been together for so long that they didn't have words for each other anymore. Brothers can be like that. During the war, their brains were like radios operating a dissident frequency. When Sam shaved, Jerry felt a phantom steel against his cheek. When Jerry stood in the front room of a whorehouse, his fist stuffed with francs, and found himself unable to betray his wife, Sam burned with a longing that could not be distinguished from shame.

PISS CLAMS: THE PISS CLAMS SHOW

They built a stage right on the beach from brightly laminated wood. The cameras arrived by helicopter. The trivia challenge formed the middle of the show, coming after the follies but before the magic. Doris and Jerry stood in one huge papier-maché clam shell, and Flo and Sam stood in another. The category was "Odds & Ends" and the question was "Under what circumstances do piss clams disgorge their humors?" "When they become unsettled," Doris said, loudly.

PISS CLAMS & I

Nobody remembers. So the cabin, a newer model, was on a trail snaking back through the low forest. They had to walk fifteen minutes to the ocean. Its hard angles gripped the barren sealight. To the right of the parking area was a primitive grill dug into the ground, and sometimes, in the morning, they found small frogs mixed in with the ashes.

PISS CLAMS: A PHILOSOPHICAL INQUIRY

Doris lay down in the foam. Each time the water slobbered onto the sand and, just as quickly, retreated, she tried to count the air bubbles. Each represented the breath of a clam. She lost count after fifty, tried again, and made it to seventy. The landscape resisted the application of such rationality, each bubble discrete and yet identical, each wave a tongue like the last but carrying some new seed: the diaphanous echo of a larval jellyfish, a kelp pod holding the deep's undersized light like a treasure.

PISS CLAMS & I

Nobody remembers, so it began with a big pot and a bigger knife. The denuded clams thickened in their own liquor as Flo and Doris split ribs of celery. Salt pork turned to a searing fat over the small stove's tooth of flame. Somehow they would make chowder, even though the amount of moisture in the air was all wrong. The filthy windows admitted a mottled light, and this too became part of it. When it was finally done, they all sat at the table and ate while the sun set, and rose, and then set again. They went to their separate bedrooms, on either side of the cabin's only hallway. The brothers slept like the dead—always had—but Flo and Doris did not sleep, and spent the night poorly, listening to the sea choke on its own voice.

PISS CLAMS: THE LONGEST NIGHT OF MY LIFE

Doris was flying. Not flying—being flown. Down on their finger of land, Flo held a string, which was tied around Doris's waist in a clump of sailor's knots. She flailed in the salt breeze like a tattered flag. Doris found a wish in her mouth—for Flo to drop the line.

GOSPELS

There are records

I.

The bell which was exiled to Siberia had no name, and so in my wisdom I gave it one: Dmitri: He of the yelping snows. Once exiled they detached his ears & tongue so he might never triangulate, again, the field of man's heart. Nonetheless he was hoisted into a steeple of frozen air by the committee of rag-women & their children, who had the long faces of dogs.

On their spines, winter's thick boot. As in a wind-bitten painting, they huddled at the doors of the church forming a many-armed desperation.

There is a note that, when struck, vibrates perfectly with the light found where our shroud of ribs is parted. The committee of rag-women & their children wanted to hear this note.

This unraveling of their stupid machines. Dmitri, deaf & dumb, bore frost.

Imagine a sheet of paper. Rising out of the middle is this village.

2.

California, as I understand it, is incorruptible. Dawn's luminous mechanism, having traveled on the breakers, leaks into an empty room with an ocean view.

The room is empty except for a birdcage (empty) & a twin bed (empty) except for the louse's many-legged marriages & a rumor of urine.

When the utterly alone finally give up and die, the brochure says, they are handled by a special division of the LAPD. Detectives turn over glum bungalows, notate the repetitious lethe-song of starved pets. When they can find no indication that anyone will come down with the madness of grief, the body and all of its stunts are cremated. Annually, Los Angeles County officiates a mass burial. Eighteen hundred people will fit in a hole the size of a small swimming pool.

This was on the radio, in a steady, cryptic rain. The travelers saw a fire through the trees, & a field reduced to a basin of light.

3.

There is another poem, in which the news is erased and rewritten.

NOTES

"Palinode" makes use of the legend of the Golem of Prague.

De proprietatibus rerum, or On the Properties of Things, is an early forerunner of the encyclopedia, written by Bartholomew of England in the thirteenth century.

The epigraph for "Defeat" is from C.P. Cavafy.

The sections of *"Vesper"* attributed to James Wright were not written by James Wright.

The epigraph for "Gospels" is from Robert Creeley.

ACKNOWLEDGMENTS

Grateful acknowledgement is made to the editors of *Ninth Letter*, where "Levis, Larry" and "One" first appeared, and to *DIAGRAM*, where "Palinode" and "Hibernation" first appeared.

COLOPHON

Text is set in a digital version of Jenson, designed by Robert Slimbach in 1996, and based on the work of punchcutter, printer, and publisher Nicolas Jenson.

ZACHARY HARRIS was born & raised in Pittsburgh, PA, and is still trying to write about it. He holds a BA in Creative Writing from Carnegie Mellon University & an MFA in Poetry from Cornell University. His work has appeared in *Bat City Review*, *Ninth Letter*, *Pleiades*, and *West Branch*, and honors include a residency at the Millay Colony for the Arts and a fellowship from Bucknell Seminar for Younger Poets. He currently teaches writing at the Pittsburgh Creative & Performing Arts High School, of which he is a former student.

NEW MICHIGAN PRESS, based in Tucson, Arizona, prints poetry and prose chapbooks, especially work that transcends traditional genre. Together with DIAGRAM, NMP sponsors a yearly chapbook competition.

DIAGRAM, a journal of text, art, and schematic, is published bimonthly at THEDIAGRAM.COM. Periodic print anthologies are available from the New Michigan Press at NEWMICHIGANPRESS.COM/NMP.

www.ingramcontent.com/pod-product-compliance
Lightning Source LLC
Chambersburg PA
CBHW031436040426
42444CB00006B/831